A WORD FROM THE LORD

RANDY C. BRODHAGEN

A WORD FROM THE LORD

Copyright © 2006 by Randy C. Brodhagen

ISBN: 0-9770398-6-2

Published by

LIFEBRIDGE

BOOKS
P.O. BOX 49428
CHARLOTTE, NC 28277

Printed in the United States of America.

CONTENTS

INTRODUCTION

I wish I could take credit for writing this book; however, the words are not mine—they were delivered *through* me by the Lord, Himself.

As a minister of the Gospel, I continually ask God to allow me to be a vessel of communication from the Father to His people.

The title of this book, *A WORD FROM THE LORD,* is exactly what you are about to receive. These messages were given under the inspiration of the Holy Spirit and spoken publicly to our congregation.

The Lord speaks for a reason—and I believe this book contains a word especially for you. Receive it with an open heart and act upon it with a willing spirit.

The Lord is saying:

For the sound of singing will be heard.
The dance of the Lord will be seen as the people
are rejoicing in My presence.
The horn will be sounded, the tambourines
will play, and the drums will roll, for the
sound of the Lord will be heard.

*The downcast spirit will begin to
rise. The mind will flow and they will
know they are in My presence.
Rise up and be strong and rejoice
in the Lord all the day long.
Be happy, be glad, be confident.
Do not lean to your own understanding.
So let your spirit flow, and let your
mind relax and rejoice.
Everything of the world (people,
nations, cities, concerns) takes a second
place to Me, saith the Lord.
Give it to Me and be glad.
Your prayer, your labor is not in vain.
Hidden things will be revealed.
They will not be hidden anymore.*

BRING GLORY TO MY NAME

My Spirit is moving to and fro throughout the earth. I am looking for My people to rise up and praise Me, to honor and give Me glory, for I am the Creator.

When people obey what I have said, it brings glory to My name.

Believe and ask; and you shall receive. Seek and you will find, knock and *believe* Me and obey. That brings glory to My name. Then I extend My hand and show My glory.

Enter into My rest, My joy, My refreshing. Those who stay in My presence—I will answer them.

The time is short. Run fast with Me. Whatever you need, receive.

———

God declares in His Word, *"The days are coming...when I will send a famine through the land—not a famine of food or a thirst for water, but a famine of hearing the words of the Lord. Men will stagger from sea to sea and wander from north to east, searching for the word of the Lord..."* (Amos 8:11-12).

What you are about to read is an answer for such a hunger—a prophetic word directly from heaven. It is exactly what is needed in these days of terror and travail.

Why does God use earthly vessels to deliver His message? It is because, *"... everyone who prophesies speaks to men for their strengthening, encouragement and comfort"* (1 Corinthians 14:3).

Since these prophetic words were given audibly, let me recommend that you find a place alone and read the chapters aloud. I believe you will be moved into the very presence of God.

It is my prayer that on these pages you will find encouragement, direction and counsel from the Lord. I believe His spiritual guidance will give you faith and hope for your future.

– *Randy C. Brodhagen*

ONE

I HAVE SET YOU APART

You are to be holy to me because I,
the Lord, am holy, and I have set you apart
from the nations to be my own.
– LEVITICUS 20:26

Fear not; only believe, and you shall see it come to pass.

For I have said unto you in time past that I am with you. When I say I won't leave you, I mean what I say. I am there. I am here. I am everywhere, but specifically I am with you.

I am with those who call upon Me, seek Me, and believe Me. I will help you, and I will deliver you in the day of trouble, in the day of trial and testing. I will show Myself mighty on your behalf.

YOU ARE GROWING

My ways are not your ways, but your ways are

9

becoming My ways, for you are growing.

Say to yourself, "I am growing in the Lord." As you speak forth this word of faith, you will see My increase come, for I am with you as I said. You will boldly say, "The Lord is my helper. Yes, the Lord is *my* helper. Of whom and what shall I ever be afraid?"

But understand this, you are My helper too, for I have called you to help Me and to take My love to the nations. My Spirit is flowing upon you, in you, and through you even now. My Spirit desires to use you to My glory. For I am with you.

YOU ARE MY AMBASSADOR

As I bless you, it is a testimony to others that I am a good and loving God. Take My word of faith to the nations. Take My word of love, and let it not just be words, but let it be shown forth in demonstration, in deeds of love—not done by mortal flesh, but by My Spirit.

I will do the things I say through you. When you lay your hands upon the sick, they will recover. When you speak forth in My Name, I will do what you say. For what you speak on earth, I will honor in heaven. I will cause great and wonderful things to come to pass through you. So call upon Me, and I will answer you, and I will show you what to say and what to do.

In Jesus' name I hear your prayer. I answer, and respond. I will do what you ask in My name, for you represent Me on this earth. I am your Lord. You are

My ambassador.

I have sent you on a mission,
On a purpose, on a plan.
I have told you to go throughout the land.
Tell the people how great the Lord is:
How good, how loving, how caring.
Demonstrate that word, for I will confirm it
With signs and wonders following.
They will know what you say is true
Because I am true in you.
When I say I set My love upon you
As an everlasting love,
It is just that. It is everlasting.
It is from above.

YOU ARE MY ROYAL PRIESTS

The earth knows nothing of My love, except it be shown. That is why I came. That's why I gave Myself a name: Jesus. I shall save My people from their sins and from what has separated them from Me. I will heal, deliver, restore, and renew them. They will rejoice again in Me. That is what I will do for you and through you, for I mean what I say.

Humble yourself in My presence, and in due season I will exalt you. I will cause My plan and blessing to come forth. All will know that I, the Lord your God,

11

did it. For you will not take credit, nor do you desire to do so. Your heart is for Me—that I receive all the glory, praise, thanks, honor and love.

This is why you are so blessed. You want Me to be honored, exalted and loved.

This is why I have set you apart, for you are My royal priests and My chosen generation, that you might show forth My praises in the earth so people might see the good works which you do by My Spirit, and give glory to My name.

ENJOY THE MOMENT

Continue, for you are growing. You are coming in to all I have fashioned and prepared. Be excited in your heart, anticipate, and look forward to what I have prepared before you. Enjoy My presence.

Allow Me to occupy your time with gladness of heart, every moment of every day, no matter what comes your way. Enjoy the moment I have prepared for you, and no matter what is happening around you, know that I am in control, saith the Lord. I reign.

REAP THE HARVEST

I have planted, I have sown, and I will reap, saith the Lord. I will reap where I have sown. My planting will produce great and abundant fruit, for My Spirit even now is moving. What I have sown will come to harvest, and you will know that I am the One who planted you. I am the One who cares for you. I am the

One who looks out for you.

I am the husbandman who takes care of the plants, who tends the vineyard, the orchards and the fields. For the harvest is ripe, and it is ready.

Go into My harvest and reap what I have sown. The time is now. I am bringing all things to fulfillment for the greatest harvest that has ever happened on the face of the earth.

My Spirit is moving, and it is drawing. Yes, I am causing people to think about Me. They will not look to another when they come to know Me and the genuineness of My love.

KEEP YOUR THOUGHTS ON ME

Go forth in My name. I empower you by My Spirit. Do good. Destroy the work of the devil, for I am with you, and I will help you. You will see that wherever you are, whatever you are doing, I will use you in that place as you are available to My Spirit.

Just keep your thoughts on Me, for then I am able to flow through you. I will cause My thoughts to be your thoughts.

I will give you peace and joy. Goodness and mercy will follow you all the days of your life. You will dwell with Me in My house forever. Look not to another. Look to Me.

SPEAK WITH CONFIDENCE

Learn to make bold confessions of faith. This is when you say, "Nothing is too difficult for My Father in heaven. Nothing is too difficult for My God to do." Then boldly speak it forth; don't be concerned what others think.

Speak boldly the promises of God.
Speak them night and day,
And speak them aloud.

You will see them, for I will do what you speak in My name. You will see them come to pass, saith the Lord.

"LET THERE BE"

I will give the nations to those who ask. You are not asking for you, but for Me. What you speak you will see come forth. As I spoke when I created, I said, "Let there be," and then I said what was to be. It started with a bold confession.

Tell sickness or disease, "Leave," and it will leave. Speak healing, and healing will come. What you speak will be what you will receive. That's why many people have not. They have not spoken what I would have them speak.

If you want life, speak life. Call it forth. You are not speaking something I have not given. You will call it forth, and it will be.

14

Speak, hear, listen and believe that what you speak in My name will become. It will happen and you will see it. For I have spoken it boldly.

This I Will Do

What do wish for? What do you desire? What do you long for? Speak it forth, and that I will do. Have I not promised whatever you ask in My name, I will do? Whatsoever things you desire when you pray, believe you will receive, and you will see it.

Have faith in God. Say to the mountain, "Move," and believe what you say will happen. If you don't doubt in your heart but believe what you say will happen, you will see it.

I say, "Come," and all things come. I say, "Go," and all things go. I say to the evil, "Go." I say to the good, "Come." Speak it forth boldly in My name, and you will see it if you believe and do not doubt.

Your answer is on the way from the Heavenlies, even as I speak.

TWO

I WILL GIVE YOU HOPE AND EXPECTATION

My soul, wait thou only upon God;
for my expectation is from him.
– PSALM 62:5 KJV

A sorrow has been upon many of My people, saith the Lord, a sorrow in the form of regrets over former things that have happened, over choices which have been made.

But I say to you today the former things are passed away. They are finished, and a new work I have begun.

You say, "I missed my opportunity. I have disobeyed what God gave me, and I didn't do it."

I will give another opportunity, and another and another. I know your heart, saith the Lord. Your heart is to love Me; it is to do good. I will cause you not to be afraid, not to regret, not to despair, thinking, "How can the Lord use me now for I have not done what I was supposed to do?"

I love you and I am working with you. I can change

17

the heart, and I can change the mind. The mind gets in the way of hearing My voice, of making My decisions.

Many of the things I have for you are not natural to you. I choose the uncommon and the unnatural for My purpose to be accomplished, so you will give Me the glory.

LET ME SPEAK THROUGH YOU

Know today that when I say to speak, you simply speak. I will give you the words to say. They will not be there until you speak; then they will come. It will not be you speaking; it will be Me speaking through you.

Yes, I have given talents and abilities. I have given aptitudes and desires. They cannot be fulfilled but by My Spirit. Except I do it through you, these are nothing more than good wishes, good desires and good talents. I make what's good excellent.

Many times, my people have leaned on their own understanding. Then the words, actions and desires were not there. They love Me with all their hearts, but they don't step out into the realm of My Spirit, trusting I will give the words. I will give the actions.

Allow Me to flow through you.

IT WILL COME TO PASS

Establish the target and do not deviate. Focus time, energy and resources. Focus people. Do not faint or be discouraged.

Don't decide things are finished when they are not. Let me determine what will be and what will not be, saith the Lord. Do not go by circumstances or situations.

Set your eyes upon the Author and Finisher of your faith and I will keep you in perfect peace. For those who are in peace in Me have focus, perspective and direction. They have a plan. They will know that in time it will surely come to pass, for I make all things beautiful in their own time.

Keep your heart, your mind, your resources and your time fixed and stayed upon Me. Wait upon Me, and I will renew your strength.

THE WAY IS PREPARED

If you have strayed, seek forgiveness and I will forgive and guide. I will instruct you in the way in which you should go. I go ahead to prepare the way.

Be strong and very courageous, and know that I am with you and will help you.

Do not give up. I will help you to stand, and you will finish. You will overcome and see the crown of life and victory I have prepared for you. Not only will you see, you will possess, for I will give it to you, saith the Lord.

Hold fast to what you know is true.
I am with you,
And I will show you what to do.
Do not get discouraged.
Do not faint along the way.
Do not stray from the path.
For I am with you, and I will cause you to be blessed.
Even when you hunger and lack,

I will supply what you need,
And I will turn back
What the evil one has intended against you.
I will cause you to stand and overcome.
Know this: I am with you,
And the work will be done.
I will be glorified in it, for the work
Will bring glory to My name.
You will see it come to pass.
You will remain steadfast, unmovable,
Always abounding in every good work.
For I have called you and destined
You to such things to My glory.

I WILL BE THERE

I love you with an everlasting love, and I care for you. I am the Lord who does not change, so what I say, I will bring to pass. You will rejoice and be glad at all times, for you know that My presence will last. As I will be there, it will be there for you. Do what I give you to do, and do it with all your heart.

Rise up; it is time now to do those things. Be focused on Me.

Call upon Me in the day of trouble, and I will help you. Call upon Me in the good times, and I will rejoice with you.

STEADFAST, UNMOVABLE

I will stand with you as I always have. You will never lack for any good thing. For many come and many go.

Know this: the blessing and the crown remains for those who finish. They are the ones who will see the blessing. Stay steadfast, unmovable, always abounding in every good work, and you will know the work will succeed, and you will know that I love you and care for you.

The Word is simple, clear, pure, easy, and it is there. When you seek with all your heart, you will find.

You will find Me and receive
The blessing I have in store.
For behold I knock at the door.
For those who will open, I will come in,
And I will be with them.

They will experience My blessing and My presence, and they will understand what I am for, and what I am against. I am for the things of good and against the things that bring harm.

SPEAK LIFE

Restrain your tongue from speaking doubt and fear. When you speak blessing, that's when I come near.

Speak life, for I am a God of the living, saith the Lord. I will bring life, for you will have what you speak in My name. It will bring glory and honor to Me.

Those who honor Me I will honor. I will cause them to ride on the high places. They will see the blessing and the goodness of the Lord all their days, and they will walk and dwell with Me forever.

Set your heart and mind, not on temporal passing

21

things, for they have no power and do not remain. They have no power to tame the flesh or to cause the things of God to come to pass in your life. They are not of Me, for they change. My Word never changes.

YOU WILL HAVE HOPE

As you focus on Me and on My Word, I will remain the same, for I do not change.

You will be rooted in My love and grounded in My faith—steadfast and unmovable, abounding in every good work. You will have anticipation and expectation of the hope I have placed before you. This hope excites you and keeps you going even when you feel faint and lose heart. My hope will remain steadfast. You will rise again, for you know ahead of you lies a blessing so wonderful you can't even anticipate, expect, or understand the fullness of the joy it will bring to you.

It comes from My throne. It is My presence. It is My present to you. Holy is the Lord.

I NEVER CHANGE

Anticipate the blessings—look forward to them. The blessings only come when you seek Me, and do things My way, saith the Lord.

Those who seek Me desire to face the things of life with My Spirit and My presence, wisdom, and guidance. They are the ones who will see the glory of God.

The things of Me do not change, for I never change. I am the same yesterday, today and forever.

THREE

My Thoughts Will Be Your Thoughts

How precious to me are your thoughts, O God!
How vast is the sum of them!
— PSALM 139:17

When your heart is filled with My presence, it will never break. You will never be lonely or feel rejected again. I will occupy your time, your thoughts and your life with the blessing of My presence. You will never lack for any good thing.

In My presence is fullness of joy, life, provision and blessing—more than you could ever ask, think or dream. When you have Me in your heart, I will give you all these other things. They are My blessings which I give to those who love Me.

Because you have set your heart upon Me, I will forgive, heal, deliver, save and give you finances,

23

health, protection and long life. Nothing will ever have power over you anymore. You will never thirst again.

WE ARE ONE
Never look to another, for I will fill you with My glory forever. No more emptiness, for you will be full and content.

You will seek Me and find Me
And know that I am here.
All these other things you seek and
Have sought, they will disappear.
Out of sight, but still in the mind.
What good is it?
When your eyes are off of Me
It is futility.
But when I am your first love,
I fill your heart and mind.
I come to you in quietness, not in strife.
No, the time is sublime.
When we are together we are one
—One heart, one mind, one Spirit.
I am a jealous God. I want your
Undivided heart, mind, and attention.
I want to hear you say,
"I want You, Lord. I want You, Lord."

SEE ONLY ME

Seek Me with all your heart and I will be found. I draw near to those who draw near to Me.

When you look at poverty, just see Me and I will bring riches. When you look at violence, just see Me and I will bring peace, saith the Lord. When you look at a hurting family, just see Me. I will come and bring comfort to them.

When you see Me, you will see liberty. The anger, hostility, sickness and disease will go.

You know Me and I want you to help others know me too. Help them to look to Me as you have learned.

Where there is pain and sorrow, I will bring healing and rejoicing, as you place your confidence and trust in Me. Don't spend time looking at what you see; only see Me. I am the difference. I am the One who makes the change.

Bring in My presence and My Spirit. Speak My name boldly among the people that they may know the Lord is mighty in their midst.

The word of faith is on your tongue, in your heart, and mind, for I have given it. Speak, act and rest in Me, and be confident you will see what I see. I don't see poverty, pain, or suffering. What I see is what I'm going to do. There is nothing too difficult for Me.

See what I see and think what I think. I can make a happy home. I can give peaceful rest, saith the Lord.

I HAVE OPENED YOUR EYES

Ask the people what they want. Tell them, "The Lord can do that for you and more, if you let Him." Give them a choice, for they see no way out. Tell them there is a better path, an opportunity.

You prayed, "Open my eyes that I might see what's going on around me." Well, I have opened your eyes, saith the Lord.

Call things that be not as though they are. Hope against hope. Have faith when there's no reason to have faith. Continue to love even though it hurts, and you will see the victory, for it's already done.

They will seek Me, and I will give them My thoughts. I will show them what they need to know and what they need to do.

I WILL GIVE YOU COUNSEL

Ask for wisdom, and I will give it, saith the Lord.

Many have missed what I planned for them because they did not ask. They leaned on their own understanding and thought, "This is too big or this is too small."

Do not allow your thoughts to be based on your experience, or that of others, but think on Me and My experience. I will give Godly counsel for what I have prepared. I will show you what to do and how. I will provide and take care of you.

I WILL PERFORM MY WORK

If I give the plan, I will also make it work. You can participate, you can cooperate, but unless I perform it, this will not happen.

Except the Lord build the house, they that labor, labor in vain. They get up early, they stay up late, they run here and there, trying to accomplish My plans. I am watching and waiting for them to be still, and know that I am God. I will bring it to pass.

I am saying believe, trust, and seek Me. Do what I tell you to do, not what you think you should do. Many times your thoughts are not My thoughts, so you run on another course and do not hear Me.

What I give is for your blessing. Enjoy and take pleasure in what I supply.

I hasten to perform My word. There are influences which will try to distract you, but I want you to be there when I deliver My blessing.

I AM THE GIVER

The thief comes to set your mind and heart on things you desire rather than Me. He frustrates, tantalizes and torments to keep you away from what I have for you. So it always remains just out of your grasp.

This is why many of My people give up. They go after the blessings, not realizing that I am the giver of whatever it is they desire from Me.

Understand, these are favors I have prepared for you. But the thief comes and causes you to concentrate more on the things than on Me—more on the plan, the project, the accomplishment, the health, the finances, the peace and the joy rather than on a relationship with Me.

So, praise Me, worship Me, honor Me, love Me, and rejoice and be glad. I will do the work, saith the Lord. Again, I say, delight in Me and I will give you the desires of your heart.

I WILL NEVER LEAVE YOU

The things of life will come and go, but I am with you forever. All you need is Me. That is why I say, be not covetous and do not desire the things of earth. I will never leave you or forsake you; therefore, you can boldly say, "The Lord is my helper, I will not fear what man shall do to me."

Man always operates in the "things" realm: relationships, health, finances, achievements, having something to do to feel worthy, loved, accepted, important, or needed. All that is futility. It is emptiness and vanity. Be not covetous.

I make all things come to pass in their season. So why strive? Why not relax and enjoy? I know what I'm doing. I know what you need before you need it. I will provide, and I will take care of you, just as I said.

THANK YOU FOR SPENDING TIME WITH ME

Many run here, there, and everywhere. I'm watching. I know where you are.

Thank you for spending time with Me. There are many other things you could be doing, but you came to be with Me. Thank you, saith the Lord. I love you.

For as you seek Me, by My Spirit, I will be found. When you call, I will answer. I will show you great and mighty things that you know not of; things that are in My heart.

You know how important it is to have someone to

share with. I made you in My image and what I tell you is not about Me, but about you. I have you in my heart.

THINK ON THESE THINGS

I desire for you to come into all that I have intended, so just be patient. It is happening.

Be to yourself and others as I am to you, for I am kind. I do not get upset by your mistakes, nor should you be upset when others fail.

Be patient, be kind, for I am there for you. I will walk with you along this path until we enter into the blessing. We will see it together, for that is My purpose and My plan.

Though there are those who are against you, I am for you. What I have in store for you is more than you can imagine.

Expand, and allow Me to guide and
Lead you to places you have never been.
Do not limit yourself, for you
Won't go where you haven't gone before.
Unless you go through My door.

You must choose. Do you want to remain where you are, or go on? Be obedient and take a leap of faith.

"Well, I don't know where I'm going or what I am

30

to do," you reply.

No, you don't, but I do, saith the Lord, and I am asking you to trust Me.

Even though your fears are screaming at you and everyone around you is saying, " You can't do this," you say, "I can't, but God can. I can do all things through Christ Jesus, my Lord, who strengthens me."

Do it with all your heart, with all that is within you, and I will bless.

Let my thoughts be your thoughts. Think on these things and do them in My Name.

FOUR

SPEAK MY WORD

The grass withers and the flowers fall,
but the word of our God stands forever.
— ISAIAH 40:8

onor My Word. Honor My Spirit and the work which I do in your life.

Do not blame or bring shame. You will be profitable in My service, for you know from whence you came. You know the Name above all Names and the grace which has brought you where you are today.

Humble yourself in My presence, and I will exalt you in due season. I will show you great and mighty things.

I HAVE ORDAINED IT

Encourage others with My Word and My promise. They are rooted within your heart, so as you speak, they will stand and do mighty exploits in My Name.

As you abide in Me, and My Word abides in you,

ask whatever you will, and it will be done—and My Father will receive the glory. Yea, it shall be so.

Understand, what is accomplished in My name, by My Spirit, will remain. No one can take this away. It will stay and not change. This I have ordained and it will surely come to pass.

You will know it is for My glory
and the good of My people that I have
done these things. Speak My name. Act
upon My Word and you will see My glory displayed
and fruit come forth. For I am the
vine and you are the branches. Apart from
Me you can do nothing, but with Me
all things are possible.

MY WORD REMAINS

Rest in My Word. It will give you confidence, saith the Lord. Nothing will change my purpose. I am the Lord, and My purpose will come to pass.

When you put your faith, trust, hope and life in My Word, you will see not only what you have heard, it will become real to you.

My Word is the same today as it was yesterday. Know that it is intended for you and you will see it as you abide in Me and My Word abides in you.

Let it dwell richly in you by my Spirit: in your heart

and mind. Let My Word fill your waking and sleeping thoughts.

My Word will cause you to grow into all I have intended, so that you inherit and participate in My divine nature.

BE DOERS OF THE WORD

My Word is My Spirit, and it is life to those who receive and believe. They will see My Word come to life and they will say, "Blessed is the name of the Lord. "Holy, holy is My God."

My people will declare, "Yes, my Lord my God has loved me." They will know what they have heard about me is true.

Then My people will rise up in their spirits and tell the nations, "Great is the Lord and greatly to be praised."

I will be honored, and I will confirm the
Word with signs and wonders. I will be
glorified in the hearts of My people who call
upon My name, who keep My commandments,
who are not just hearers of the Word only, but doers.
They will be the ones who are blessed
and through whom the fruit will be displayed,
and I will reward them accordingly.

35

I AM MOVING ON THE EARTH

Loose the manifestation of My Spirit, saith the Lord. For My ways are not the people's ways. Unless they seek Me, they will not find Me. My ways are discerned by My Spirit alone.

They know nothing of My Spirit except I give understanding. Seek knowledge of My ways and My Spirit, and I will guide your path. You will never lack for any good thing, for I will supply. I will bring what I have prepared. I knew you would be here in this moment, in this time and I am waiting for you.

Before the foundation of the world, I laid out the line of time. It is now my Spirit will move through you. My Spirit desires to work mightily in your midst. This is My time to move in the earth.

Call the people to rise up in Jesus' name. Yesterday, today, and forever, I am the God who is the same.

Let it be made known there is none like Me. Listen to no other. I desire to see My glory displayed throughout the earth, to make known the presence of the living God. No other power shall be in My presence, for Mine is the glory and the power and the dominion forever and ever.

Bring My Message

You are the messenger I am sending forth. Speak my Word to the people, let them hear and know that I am God. Whether they receive or reject is not your concern. You are to bring the message, to speak the Word, and to work the works. My glory will be displayed as people believe upon My name.

You Be The One

Were there not ten healed and one came back to give thanks to God? Yes, it is so.

May you be the one who says,
"Yes, great is My God and greatly to be praised."
You be the one who proclaims
My goodness and My love.
You be the one who says,
"Yes, I am loved from above."
Yes, you be the one who displays My glory,
Who believes in Me, who trusts
In Me, who hopes in Me.
You be the one who does what I say.
Don't wait around for someone else to come.
You be the one.
You rise up in what you know is true
And watch what I will do for you.

Stand up and say,
"Yes, I believe God in this very moment
In this very day.
I believe all He has done."
Yes, you know it's true,
So tell the people what I will do.
Tell them, "Don't be ashamed, don't be afraid,
Don't be discouraged, don't be dismayed."
I keep the truth that I have expressed.
I keep My Word and they will be blessed.
I have said it, and I will do it.
I have promised, and I will fulfill.

I Am Your Confidence

Tell the people their part is to believe, receive and respond, not to reject.

Understand, the same power that raised Me from the dead is working in you. It is true this day. Be confident in Me, for I am your confidence. Be not afraid of the sudden fear or the overwhelming flood that comes.

I will be there in that moment, in that day, and by My power I will turn things away.

To the left, a thousand will fall; to the right, ten thousand will go, but it will not come near you. You have put your confidence and trust in Me. I will deliver you. I will give you long life and satisfy you with every desire and blessing by My Spirit.

You will be under My shadow, hid with Me in

God. Evil may seek you out, but it will not find you. The devourer who tries to steal the blessing I have given will not be able to find you. All he sees is Me—and he will not come around me, for he knows his destiny.

REMAIN FAITHFUL TO MY WORD

Yes, by My Spirit I use many things to do that which I have planned and purposed. It is I, the Lord that doeth these things. Look not to yourself, look not to another, for it is I who brings the blessing from the north, the south, the east, the west. I cause it to come to you.

You will be blessed as you call upon Me, as you trust in Me, as you remain faithful to Me and to my Word. Yes, these things I will do for I am the one to be adored.

FIVE

RECEIVE MY LOVE

As the Father has loved me, so have
I loved you. Now remain in my love.
– JOHN 15:9

Everything which is of Me is summed up in these
three words: faith, hope and love.

Prosper in My path, for love never fails. It is
always realized, and faith makes it happen.

- Your hope is not in yourself; you have hope
  in Me.
- Your faith is not in yourself; but you have
  faith in Me.
- Your love is not for yourself; you have love
  for Me.

These three remain when all self-serving things are
done. I have put My faith in you, I have put My hope
in you, and I have put My love in you. They remain
and do not change.

41

YOU WILL HAVE FAITH AND HOPE

Love bears all things, believes all things, hopes all things, endures all things, and never fails. Always remember love has faith and it has hope. This is why love is the greatest, because it includes all of these.

You can have faith and not have love. You can have hope, but not have faith or love. But My love gives. My faith receives. My hope gives a future. Love is now; it is here.

Please know that I never give up on you. When My love is working in your life, you will have the same compassion and won't give up on others.

PRAY OUT OF MY LOVE

When you pray, be sure you pray out of My love, for then you will be able to believe all things, hope all things, and endure all things. You will always see your prayers answered.

My love never fails. This is why I say, "If when you stand praying and you remember you have something against somebody, forgive, so your Father in heaven may forgive you."

Forgive because I have forgiven you. I have set my love upon you. So, when you pray, it is an act of My love, an act of My faith, an act of My hope, which I have placed upon you.

YOU HAVE MY HEART

When you pray out of My love, you will pray My desire, My will, My purpose and My plan. It will not be self-seeking because you will know it is My love which has enabled you to come and pray. Otherwise, I would not hear you.

The reason I do not hear the prayers of many is because they fail to pray out My Love, saith the Lord. They want their own way, not caring for those around them or about My desires.

They will fail. But when you pray out of My love, you have My heart, and I will tell you what to pray for. It will be to My glory.

It is My will for your prayers to be answered. Speak them forth, for they are the hidden things I have prepared. In My Word I call them a mystery, but they will not remain a mystery to you who seek My Glory and desire My presence.

MY LOVE WILL BE CONFIRMED

Draw near to Me, and I will draw near to you. I will show you these things that I speak even now through My son. I will confirm them within you.

I desire you to speak into this earth the things I have prepared for those who love Me and love My

43

appearing, saith the Lord. As you speak, I will give you the words to say, for it will not be you speaking; it will be Me speaking through you.

I WILL DEMONSTRATE MY GOODNESS

In the hearts of many people, their longing has been diverted, for they don't know My love. You can tell them and they will listen because they want to know about love; but until they know Me, they do not know what true love is.

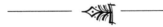

I will confirm the word which you speak with signs and wonders. I will demonstrate My love to them as I did to My children in the wilderness. Daily I showed them My love and My ways. They were unbelieving, stubborn, stiff-necked, and hard-headed; yet My unfailing love continued to demonstrate My goodness toward them, so they might believe.

THE WORD OF HOPE

When you pray out of My love, you speak the word of faith. You call things that be not as though they are, and they become; they happen. The word of hope you speak forth will give vision because you are giving plans that come from My purpose and My heart, which are always intended for My glory.

When you speak them forth, it causes My hope to abound in the earth.

Ask to know the height, the depth, the breadth, the width of My love I have for you, and I will show it to you. I will reveal Myself, for I am love, I am faith, I am hope. I Am who I Am and there is none like unto Me, saith the Lord.

CONTINUAL MIRACLES

When you seek Me with all your heart, I will be found, and you will know My love which never fails. You will demonstrate My faith and hope, and I will be glorified. The people around you will know, that God is in their midst.

What you speak and do, I will confirm. The people will know I am the Lord. You are My child and I love them through you.

Let your actions be preceded with love-prayers—love-faith and love-hope—and you will see continual miracles. For miracles are not the exception, they are the fruit of My love and compassion. They are a demonstration of My heart for My people.

*When you pray the prayer of love, your words
need not be many because they come from a heart
that is ready. It believes all things, hopes all things,
endures all things, love never fails. Yes,
My love prepares all things for miracles.*

45

IT NEVER FADES

Learn to pray the prayer of love, which I have taught you, and you will see wonderful things by My Spirit come to pass. The fruit will remain.

Don't be moved by what you see or feel. Love never fails.

I love you with an everlasting love which never fades away or changes. Hold on through faith for what you prayed and believed.

WAVES OF REFRESHING

Nothing shall separate you from My love, which I have placed upon you, and which you are now able to receive.

What you will see will be waves of refreshing flowing upon you and through you to bless people in your family, in your neighborhood, your city, your nation and the nations of the earth.

My love is being poured out in all places, to take down the walls that separate and divide, and to cause the lonely to come into community, and there to reside. They will find hope and blessing.

When you advance in My Spirit with My love, then My purpose will be accomplished. You will see

Me confirm the Word from above with My love and My power.

RECEIVE MY LOVE

Permit me to love you as I would desire, for I care for you far beyond what you can imagine or express—above what you can think or understand.

I love and honor you, for I am the Lord.

As you are obedient, you will receive all I have for you. There will be no resistance. I can freely flow.

Receive My love this day.

SIX

WALK IN MY SPIRIT

*Since we live by the Spirit, let us
keep in step with the Spirit.*
– GALATIANS 5:25

My glory will not be based upon the flesh, but upon My Spirit. So rely upon Me, not on your weakness to accomplish what I have intended.

Everything will come to naught if tried by your own effort. Wait upon Me and I will direct, guide, lead, and show you what to do and how it is to be accomplished.

If you are tired and weary, you will know you are laboring in your own flesh and by your own strength.

Come to Me for refreshing. They that wait upon Me will rise on the wings of eagles. They will run and not be weary; they will walk and not faint.

You will have strength sufficient for the day, excitement, joy, and refreshing along the way. My Spirit is at work in you.

My way is easy and My burden is light, for you are yoked up with Me. You will say, "I have tried so hard

49

to be spiritual, to do what God wants, but this is different. This is easy."

Then you will realize it is Me pulling the load and I am carrying you. Yes, you are more than a conqueror, for you are enjoying what I have conquered, you are experiencing the blessing that belongs to those who walk with Me.

BY MY MIGHT

For My people to walk by My Spirit they need the power of My words. This is why I am asking you to speak what I give you. Speak forth My life, and My power will increase—not by the power of people, but by My might, saith the Lord.

It is powerful to perform My will and perfect purpose.

Even now I am doing the work for those who place their confidence and trust in Me. It will be easy, empowered by My strength and might. By My Spirit it will be accomplished. I will create, form, guide and direct and see it unto its full completion and fruition.

The work will be finished and all will say, "The Lord has done a great and mighty thing. Yes, the Lord has achieved what He desired, and it is good. Truly, this is from God, and not of man."

Gladness of Heart

So raise your hands to Me. Lift up holy hands and bless the Lord and give Me the glory which is worthy of My name. I am great and wonderful, I am awesome in the midst of My people.

I am all power, for there is none like Me. I am the Lord of Hosts, mighty in battle, mighty in peace, mighty in rest, mighty in work. I am the Lord, and I know how to do all things well. So put your heart and mind at rest. Settle down and enjoy the time I have provided you in this life in My presence.

I desire to occupy your days with gladness of heart, not sorrows and woes, or fear and unbelief, not depression and anxiety, confusion and stress. No, I long to fill your days with happiness. So rejoice, be glad in Me and be blessed.

———— ⚜ ————

Rest in My plan.
Rest in my ways, having confidence
your life is in My hand.
Trust Me, trust Me, and trust Me some more.
Yes, I am the Lord whom you adore.
You will rejoice, and you will be glad,
And yes, you will say,
"This is the day that the Lord has made,
I will be glad.
I have put away sadness of heart,

51

To receive the gladness of heart
That My Lord has supplied."
You will say, "Yes, I believe in God."

USE YOUR FAITH

Your faith in Me will not go away empty. You will never be ashamed or confounded. You will not depart dismayed, despairing, depressed, deprived, or depraved. Know that your faith in Me is certain.

I am the Lord who gave you the faith which you now possess. Use it, knowing I the Lord your God will do what I have said. I am the Lord, and I do not lie.

BE STRONG IN ME

I will pour out My Spirit even more, for as people receive strength from Me, I will increase in their midst in even greater and mightier ways.

So draw near to Me. Set your heart and your mind upon Me, and I will keep you in perfect peace. I will guide, lead, direct, instruct, correct, and I will bless. You will decrease and I will increase.

Great rejoicing will be heard instead of terror and discord. The people will know, yes, the Lord is in their midst. Where I am is fullness of joy, life, blessing, gladness, peace and hope. Yes, hope in God, and you will give Me the praise.

You will see the increase as I have promised, for you will have your delight in Me.

I am the One who gives you courage. Be strong in

Me and in the power of My might. Put on the whole armor of God that I have supplied and given, for it will keep you in the day of evil and you will overcome.

THE BLESSING WILL INCREASE

Learn to flow with My Spirit and I will bring your thoughts to perfect peace. You will hear My still voice say, "This is the way. This is the way."

Let not your heart be troubled; don't be afraid. This is the path I have prepared. You see the blessing of God for yourself, for your children, and for your children's children. And the blessing will increase from generation to generation.

All the good things you have believed, you will see.

A NEW SONG

By My Spirit, I will give you a new song—a love song. You will sing it all your days. As I have loved you, you will love Me.

It is a song of thankfulness, adoration, admiration. I have taken you out of the mire, and I have given you a good new life. You are thankful, for you triumph in Me at all times, in all occasions.

Everywhere you go, whatever you're doing, I will be the center of your communication and the center of

your conversation. Your adoration of Me will come
forth from your lips, for I have set those words in your
heart and in your mind. You were born to praise Me,
and you were born to worship Me, saith the Lord.

Serve, love, and care for My people, for I am coming
soon. Surely goodness and mercy shall follow you all
the days of your life and you will dwell in the house of
the Lord forever.

My Mercy and goodness
Have covered your past.
I have given you new hope and a future,
And they will last.
Remain in My love.
Do not let criticism or negativity
Come into your spirit.
Listen not to the evil report that comes around.
It will take your eyes off of Me
And cause you not to soar in the heavens,
But fall upon the ground.
The dirt is the dirt; the sky is the sky,
The heavens are the heavens, and that is no lie.
You were born to soar with Me.

BY MY SPIRIT
Do not allow yourself to be caught up in self pity,
negligence, disobedience, unbelief, fear, doubt, and
woe, for they are not of you anymore. No, they are low

and you are high.

Set your mind upon things above, on the things that are of Me, and not on the things below.

You are risen with Me and positioned with Me on high. Look not beneath, for you are higher. For My Spirit and My life rest within you and upon you.

There is nothing too hard or difficult for Me. Lift your heart and mind and set them upon Me, for I am high and lifted up.

It is not by might, nor by power, but by My Spirit, saith the Lord.

SEVEN

I AM
YOUR SUPPLY

*...whoever drinks the water I give him will never
thirst. Indeed, the water I give him will become in
him a spring of water welling up to eternal life.*
– JOHN 4:14

D o not say, "I lack," or "I do not have enough."
Understand, what I supply is all you need. It will
satisfy and fulfill.

There was a time when you said the plate was not
full enough, but I say to you, "Behold, I have a better
way." I provide all that is needed.

Look not at what you do not have. I am with you
now, and I will be with you in your future. I am all you
require.

As I have helped countless others, I will assist you.

"FATHER, I KNOW YOU HEAR ME."

My Son, Jesus, took what I supplied and provided.
He believed Me and thanked Me. I took what He had

and multiplied it. Many were blessed through Him as He walked the earth. I was with Him, and I helped Him.

He knew that whatever He asked, I would do. He never requested anything I did not want Him to ask, for He sought Me first before He did or said anything.

I honored His request as He said, "Father, I know You hear Me always."

Today, I will always listen as you call upon me with a pure, believing, faithful heart. I will answer and do great and wonderful things for you.

Do you believe this? If so, put aside your fear, discontent, confusion, worry and anxiousness.

DON'T BE MOVED BY FEAR

The pressures of life do not come from Me. They are from the thief, from others, and from those you induce yourself. You must learn to say, "No. I will do the work in the Lord's time when He makes a way." It will be the right time.

During these days, I will take care of you, saith the Lord. Do not yield to pressure, but be led by My Spirit.

Don't be moved by guilt, fear, or what others might think of you. Do not worry over your reputation or your life; be concerned about nothing.

58

Have you not read how I take care of the birds of the air and the lilies of the field? They have no cares, but enjoy what I do in them, through them, to them and for them. They take no thought of tomorrow.

Are you not of more value than all of these? Be not of little faith, but increase your faith. Trust in Me. Be moved by My Spirit.

PRAISE ME!

When everything seems to be going wrong, pray in the Spirit, not with your understanding, for your understanding is leading you into fear, worry and anxiousness.

*You don't see what I am going to do
or how I will accomplish it. That is why you
must trust Me and act upon the right things
I have shown you from My Word.*

When you do not know what lies ahead, begin to praise Me.

If the blind leads the blind, they both fall into the ditch. Is it not better that I lead and guide? I know the steps and can prepare the way when you don't know which path to take.

Do not be concerned with what others have or have not done. You can only change circumstances if I give you the ability.

DIE TO YOURSELF

There were times when I gave you much and other times when you had nothing. Is your provision based on what you see? Or is it based upon Me?

My son, Paul, had an understanding of life. He said, "I have learned the secret to being content no matter what state I am in, whether I'm abounding in much, I have nothing, or I have little. I've learned to be content."

He knew My Son lived, died and rose for him. This was the message he proclaimed to the people.

Die to yourself and live in the resurrected life in the power of God, which I have prepared for you, saith the Lord.

When everything seems dead, it just looks that way. I am a God of the living, and I can bring what's dead back to life.

I AM MORE THAN PROVISION

People have a difficult time with change, for they do not understand what they have is fleeting. Life is short. Relationships take only a small amount of our span of time.

Grass grows and then withers. Flowers come up and they fade and disappear. Then the next year arrives and they enjoy again what I supply.

Why can't people enjoy what they have, while they have it, rather than worrying how long it will remain?

I am with you always. That's all you need to know. I will guide and lead you, as you permit Me to love and bless your life with every good thing.

I am more than provision; I am true life.

BELIEVE ME

The ways of My Spirit are uncommon to people's natural thinking. I say, "Believe, and you will see." People say, "See, and then I'll believe."

Such a vew will never reveal what I have prepared, for doubt will not allow My blessing to be visible.

What they see will decrease and perish. The unbeliever will gather crops, but they will never be enough.

They will never be satisfied, for they are not fulfilled within themselves. It would not matter how much they had, they would never be complete, whether in relationships, finances, health, peace or joy; they will not have enough.

Only I, saith the Lord, can fulfill and bring contentment, peace and gratitude for what you have. Only I can bring enjoyment and rejoicing in your heart. I am the key to an abundant life.

MY BLESSINGS NEVER CEASE

Life does not consist in what you possess, or in your health, wealth or popularity. It is found only in Me.

So whether you are rejected or loved does not matter. Your life is in Me. If you have wealth or have nothing, it is not important, for I am your life.

Isn't that all you need?

People have not been taught My ways,
so they do not understand. They think,
"God is with Me if I'm popular." Or,
"God is with me if I have health."

One day success is here and the next day it is gone. The world needs to know My blessings never cease.

TRUST ME

Be not like my servant, Jonah, who was not happy to see what I did; who was more concerned with his own comfort, his own life.

When I grew the plant that covered him and gave him shade, he was pleased. But when the plant withered and died, he was filled with woe.

Even though I used Jonah for My glory and thousands of people were saved, he continued to complain.

Be not like him, for he based his comfort on his own desires.

I did not listen to his complaints, since I had a purpose for his life.

Do not be concerned when all other avenues are shut off. There's something I want you to learn, and a destiny to be fulfilled. Trust me, then step out in faith.

Don't be upset at Me, for I only have good plans for you. I only desire to see you come into My presence with joy and thanksgiving forever.

You don't "need to know" how I will accomplish My purpose. Just believe Me and step out in My Spirit. Know that I have already gone ahead and prepared the way for you. Believe Me, and you will see My hand at work.

I will supply your needs.

EIGHT

I WILL GIVE YOU STRENGTH

*It is God who arms me with strength
and makes my way perfect.*
– PSALM 18:32

You will rise up in confidence and courage. Despair will flee from you, for you will know the strength of the Lord is upon you, the boldness of the Spirit of the Living God.

You will know this is the day which the Lord has made. Your feelings will fade that are contrary to My name, and you will say, "I will rejoice and I will be glad."

The weak will say, "I am strong in the Lord."

As they praise Me, My strength will rise upon strength, faith will rise upon faith, courage will rise upon courage. They will soar above every situation and circumstances on earth.

I AM YOUR STABILITY

I will establish My kingdom forever, in peace, joy,

65

love and righteousness. The people will proclaim, "Yes, the Lord has done great and wonderful things in our midst. Yes, the Lord is mighty. He is who He says He is, and He has done what He says He will do. Yes, it is true."

I will make the situations and circumstances
Of the earth according to My plan.
I will destroy the work of the evil one in the land.

So, let everyone who calls My name and who is called by My name rejoice and be glad, for I am the same and I never change.

Let stability be found in this earth where there is none. This stability is in Me, saith the Lord. I give the ability to respond, to be responsible and give an account.

You will say, "Yes, what a privilege it is to take what the Lord has given to me, use it for His glory, and then to give myself back to Him."

MY PRESENCE WILL BE WITH YOU

You will stand strong in My Spirit and not back down. The joy of My strength will be upon you. The delight of My presence will be with you, for you long to enter into My courts with praise.

Thanksgiving is on your lips each day. You rejoice in Me, for you know I am the One who loves you with an everlasting love that never fades away or changes. Yes, I am the Lord, your God. There is none like Me.

PUT AWAY ANGER

Call upon Me in the day of trouble, and I will show Myself mighty. Whatever comes against you I will help, enable, cause you to stand and bring glory to My name.

As you begin to praise and worship Me, My Spirit will rest and bring you peace.

Let not your heart be troubled, neither be afraid. Put anger away, for it comes with frustration when you are operating in your own strength.

BE UNITED

Stand fast together. As you are united in My Spirit, one will move a thousand, and two will move ten thousand. Together we will see the blessing.

Today hold the hand of another as I hold
your hand, saith the Lord. I will bind and knit
you together with others all over the earth,
for you are one in Spirit, one in heart.

Do not let any selfish desire separate you from one another. Put aside any misunderstanding or misguided direction—let it not divide you.

Stand together in My Spirit and seek Me with all your heart. When two or three are touching any one thing, I will cause great and wonderful things to happen.

You will know the goodness of My Spirit upon you. Nothing can defile you any longer, for I will separate what will not repent and return to My ways. It will be removed from My midst.

Those who call upon Me and yield to Me will I cleanse. They will be pure before Me.

THE NATIONS WILL TREMBLE

I am calling My people to unity and strength this day throughout the land. My holiness will bring terror to those who terrorize, for they will be afraid of Me.

I will stand mighty in behalf of My people who call upon My name. All that is not of My Spirit will run in fear before Me. They will no longer laugh and mock.

No longer will they be an abomination before Me. I will cause these things to cease in My presence.

They will know that I am the Lord. All the nations of the earth will fear and tremble before Me.

LOOK TO MY SPIRIT

My time is short. Be about My purpose and stand

together. It is not time to pull away.

Look not to your own interest but prefer the interests of My Spirit. I will bless those who honor Me, who put faith and trust in Me, and who are about My purpose.

This is not a time for the weak to be weak, but to come to Me and be made strong.

I have not placed within you a spirit of timidity or fear, but of power, love, and a sound, well-balanced, disciplined mind controlled by My Spirit.

This is not oppression, but the ability to bless others through you.

I Will Deliver You

Have you felt weakness and failing strength? Have you gone through doubt in the valley of the shadow where you could not see?

I am there. Take Me by the hand, believe my promise and I will see you through. Many are the afflictions of the righteous, but I deliver you out of them all. Not some, but all!

During these times, stir up My gift within you. Fan the flame. Energize and build yourself up in the most holy faith, praying in the Holy Ghost.

Be bold in the Spirit. Be strong in the Lord, and in the power of His might. Don't back down. When you stand, I will stand with you.

SPEAK FROM YOUR HEART

Do not be double-minded. Look not at the ups and downs and the reports that you hear. Look at the finish. That's what you are to speak.

Nothing I have planned shall be impossible to you. Don't speak from your head, but from your heart.

Get rid of any strife. There must not be unforgiveness or bitterness. Seek forgiveness as you are forgiven. Guilt will hinder you in the evil day. It will be used against you by the enemy, and he will say, "Do you remember when you did that?" He is the accuser of the brethren.

Be not ignorant of his ways. For in the evil day he will use these things against you so that you are not standing sure.

STAND FIRM

Persevere in the faith. Some things you must work toward and endure. Be patient and hold fast to what you know is true.

What I have set before you, no one can take away. It is yours. Don't give it up. Stand firm. There is no giant in the land that I am not bigger than.

Be rooted and grounded in the faith, and you will stand, overcome and see the victory of the Lord.

Stand in awe. Stand in reverence. Stand in praise. Stand in worship of an Almighty, loving God.

Be sober. Be vigilant. Don't be found unprepared.

Do you think the evil one comes at a time you expect him? No, he's a thief who comes to steal, to kill, to devour and destroy. He looks and waits for a more opportune time, when you let down your guard and you are not standing at your post—when you are relaxed and unaware.

I WILL BE YOUR CONFIDENCE

Be prepared. Don't be drunk with the things of the world or take your eyes off of Me. Focus, and you will stand in that day.

When he comes, be watching and praying so you will not fall into temptation. Your spirit is willing and the flesh will be weak, but you can rely upon My Spirit in that time, saith the Lord.

It doesn't matter what comes against you. I have overcome all things. I am the greater one who is within you, greater than anything you will ever face or deal with in this life.

I will be your confidence. I will be your strength.

NINE

MY BLESSINGS
WILL NEVER CEASE

*For I will pour water on the thirsty
land, and streams on the dry ground; I will
pour out my Spirit on your offspring, and
my blessing on your descendants.*

—ISAIAH 44:3

I move in hearts in different ways, but all will know My Spirit and My presence. What you need will manifest within you.

For some it will be joy and laughter, for others peace, confidence, worthiness, humility, or a deep sense of thankfulness.

As My Spirit moves, I will give you what you need at the appointed time. If you need encouragement, I will bring you encouragement. If you require healing in your mind, that I will do. If you want healing in your body, you will receive it. If you need patience, My patience will rise within you, for I move in the moment.

First I provide freedom and liberty so that you are able to enjoy what I have to give.

MY SPIRIT IS NOT LIMITED

You have heard Me say when I was asked what My name is, "I Am Who I Am." You have heard My Son declare, "I am the bread of life. I am the resurrection and the life, I am the way, the truth and the life."

He said who He is—and what He can do. Today I am doing the same for you.

I Am Who I Am. To some I am peace, to others, joy, salvation, deliverance or wisdom. When My presence is manifest, I show Myself differently to each one, even in the same place. My Spirit is not limited by location, situations or circumstance. I am All in All.

WHAT DO YOU SEEK?

I am everything you need. If you need provision, I will provide. If you need understanding, I will understand. You need not look to another.

What is it you seek? I will fill the emptiness of your heart, the loneliness of your mind. I will give you plans and purpose.

Worship Me, praise Me, speak to Me, love Me, call My name, and I will be there.

Do not think you are unworthy; ask for more.

When you welcome My presence,
Forgive and forget.
I show mercy, and not neglect.
You do not make yourself worthy,
That is for Me to do.

Ask me to bless you and I will. As you go out into the world, I will bless others through you. Do not hesitate to request of Me more blessing: spiritually, mentally, emotionally, physically, and in relationships.

I Have Already Given

When My blessing falls, you will receive My grace and the ability for mental creativity and financial increase. As you are blessed, you will have resources to touch the lives of others.

People continue to ask, "Oh Lord,
help my finances, help my relationships,"
when all along it is I who have already given
the ability to have blessed relationships, to
have blessed finances, the ability to
acquire wealth, and good health.

When you think you are cursed and unworthy, you condemn all around you. You only do what you believe, and if you believe you are cursed, then you speak cursing. If you believe you're blessed, you will speak blessing.

I WILL REKINDLE THE FIRE

I am mighty in your midst, and I am with you. In those days when you were distracted and walked in your own selfish ways, my Spirit was still with you. I did not forsake you, for I am the Lord, your God who loves you with an everlasting love.

Even now, I draw you to Myself. I will rekindle the holy fire which changes lives, hearts, actions and thoughts. But you will not see the consuming fire which is coming upon the rest of the earth—a flame that destroys.

Set your heart and mind on the better path I have prepared for you. My pleasures will be beyond anything you could ever desire or long for. They are forever—everything else is temporary, only lasting for a season.

STIR UP THE GIFT

My blessing is upon you wherever you go: blessed in the city, blessed in the country, blessed coming in, blessed going out.

Allow My Spirit to fill you to overflowing and you will know whatever you ask in My name I will do.

You will see that which you speak in My name come to pass.

Stir up the gift of God which I have placed within you. Rise up in My Spirit, for I will give you utterance about things that you know not of.

You will speak by My Spirit, who knows what is needed to be done in the earth.

YOU WILL OVERFLOW

Be not afraid of sudden fear when it appears, for I shall be your confidence. Your blessing is on the way.

I will take you out of the whirlwind, out of the confusion, out of the despair and hopelessness. I will settle you down and enable you to be planted—steadfast, unmovable, always abounding in every good work.

You will begin to see things as I see them. They are possible and will happen. In the quietness of your heart you will begin to sense a strength you know not of. It comes from my Spirit and is part of the blessing I give.

My child, you will not fear, regardless of what man shall do. I will be your confidence in that very hour.

You will overflow with my blessing and be a shining light for all to see. Out of you will flow living waters by My Spirit—living thoughts, living words, and living deeds which will bring glory to My name.

A NEW WAY

Abide in Me, and let My Word abide in you. You will desire My presence more than anything else, for that is what you will long for. Even what you once delighted in will satisfy no more—what I provide will be far greater.

In all areas of life, I will guide you in wisdom. You will have no lack and you will not desire to return to the former things, because I give to you a new and a living way.

A resurrected life, a life of power.
A life of provision, a life of generosity,
caring and sharing,
A life that no longer seeks its own.
A life that wants to give.
As I have given freely to you,
Give freely to those who I place in your life.
I am sending them to you.
You love them as I love them.
You care for them as I care for them.
They will find great peace and joy in your presence,
My presence will be in that place,
For you delight in Me.
You will talk of Me. You will share about Me.

You will work My works, for we are one,
saith the Lord.
Whatever you ask in My name I will do for you.
You will see the glory that I will display,
For I will always do what you say.

YOU WILL TELL THE NATIONS

By loving Me you have released freely all I possess. You will see it on every side and say to others, "My life is so blessed. My God is so wonderful— so loving, kind, patient and understanding."

You will boast about Me to the nations, and tell them:

"Oh, come and see and taste
How good the Lord is.
Participate in His love.
Receive His goodness that
He has for you from above.
Open your heart, open your mind
To all that He has for you."
You will say, "He is good, He is true.
Come and see for yourself.
What He's done for me,
He will do it for you."

TEN

REST IN MY PEACE

*Peace I leave with you; my peace I give you. I
do not give to you as the world gives. Do not let
your hearts be troubled and do not be afraid.*
— JOHN 14:27

My peace I give to you, not as the world gives.
I invite you to enter in, for the song of deliverance is
the song of rest.

- My peace brings healing.
- My peace brings refreshing.
- My peace brings hope.
- My peace brings joy.
- My peace brings confidence.
- My peace brings life.
- My peace brings salvation.

NO MORE STRIVING

Receive what is mine, for I only give good and
perfect gifts to those I love. You are My own, saith the

Lord. Accept and receive.

You will never lack for any good thing in My presence. You will not be intimidated, harassed or forced, for I do not work in such a way. You will be led by My peace day after day.

It will be given to all who accept and receive what I offer, for I am gentle and kind to the unlovable, the unloving, and the despised.

I change those who come to Me. When My peace falls upon them and enters their lives, they will never be the same, for rest will be theirs.

They will not want again: No more striving, competing, unworthiness or superiority, for these contribute nothing to My peace. In My presence they are of no value.

NO MORE CONDEMNATION

You will be blessed on every side. My rest will be upon you and you will know My presence.

My joy and hope will be there. My life, love and forgiveness will be yours. There will be no more condemnation or shame. Never again will there be anything you need to hide from others. All will be open before Me.

LET THEM GO

Release those things which have troubled you. Let

them go. My peace I give to you; all else is not yours.

I do not give you anything but peace,
saith the Lord.
Know this and let your cares go.
For they have caused you nothing but woe.
Let them go.

Say, "I let go of the pain. I let go of the hurts. I let go of the anger. I let go of the bitterness. I let go of the vengeance. I let go of the despair. I let go of the helplessness, and the clinging, trying to be loved, and the ravages of failure."

For My peace to have effect, saith the Lord, you have to turn loose of all else.

I WILL FILL THEIR HEARTS

Those who come to Me will find I am all they need. They don't require accolades, or to be recognized, loved and accepted. They need only Me and My presence, for My peace will fill their hearts with all they desire.

Joy will surround them, for My peace and happiness go together. They will know they can rest in Me and welcome My presence. They can enjoy Me and all the blessings I have placed in their lives—the people and provisions I supply by My gracious hand.

A PLACE OF REST

You will rest forever in My glory. My joy and My life will be with you. I will not leave you. I am a God of the living, not the dead.

You will never die in Me, nor will hope ever die in you. I have good plans for your future. Rest confidently in Me, and let My Spirit come upon you. Let it bring you comfort.

Call upon Me and realize I am here. You are not alone, nor will you ever be. My glory, My peace and My presence is upon you.

Others are wandering aimlessly, feeling rejected. They don't know what to do. Encourage them to anchor their faith in Me and they will wander no more. They will know they have a place of rest, peace and hope.

The world cannot have My peace because it does not know Me. It seeks its own way, but it is not My way.

I will abide, faithful and true,
And it is all for you.
I will refresh and comfort you.
You will have strength sufficient for the day.
And you will overcome.
You will see the mighty hand of
your God deliver you.
You will see that My praise

Will be shown forth from your life.
You will be free from strife.
You will be at peace again.
You will know the goodness of the Lord within.
You will know it in your heart.
You will know it in your mind.
The former things have passed away
And the new things have come.
The old is no more, and the new has begun.
So rejoice this day, saith the Lord.
In my presence is fullness of joy
And life everlasting.
So rejoice and be encouraged in this hour.
For this is the time to see your God's power.

I WILL BRING LIFE

Pour out your life as I have poured out My life for you. Do you understand if you seek to save your life, you will lose your life? If you lose your life for My sake, you will gain your life.

When I say pour out your life, understand what I mean. It is no longer you who lives, but it is Me living in you, and the life you live is only by the faith of the Son of God.

My Spirit is upon and in you. For this reason, when you pour out your life to others you are pouring Me out upon them, and that will bring life.

I am living water. They will never, ever thirst again. My words are Spirit and life and this is what you will

85

impart as you speak. My Spirit will turn darkness into light, it will turn poverty into wealth, it will turn confusion into understanding, and it will turn anxiety into peace.

NO MORE DOUBT

Cast aside the cares, the worries and the fears, for they do not profit you or bring peace. They are not of faith, nor a part of Me.

Doubt, unbelief and insecurity have no place in your life. They have no right upon your thoughts or no reason to be in your presence.

I do not desire what is not of faith, the things which do not allow Me to share My grace or allow Me to show Myself strong.

I love you, saith the Lord, and I have the ability to do what I say I will do. Receive, believe, and you will see the glory of your God manifest before your eyes.

I DELIGHT IN YOU

Yes, child, you are Mine. I will not allow another to hurt, harm, oppress or abuse you. I am your God who loves you with an everlasting love. I forgive you. I care for you. I delight in you. I find you as My joy, and My precious one. I love you.

Receive My love and know that in those moments,

when you are fulfilling My plans, I am with you. I will help you as you call upon Me. I will be there.

WORDS OF COMFORT

Delight in Me and lift your heart. If you want to sing, sing. If you want to dance, dance. Rejoice in My presence and My peace will last.

My glory is here with you now. When you understand this you will see how I work all things out to your good and to My glory. Forever I will be praised. I will bless you, saith the Lord, and you will see goodness of life now and for eternity.

Let these words bring comfort to your heart. Let them bring peace to your life forever.

ELEVEN

ENCOURAGE MY PEOPLE

Preach the Word; be prepared in season and out of season; correct, rebuke and encourage—with great patience and careful instruction
– 2 TIMOTHY 4:2

There are times when those I love are pressured by their own concerns and desires. So children, comfort My people, encourage them in faith and help then walk in My ways.

Never give up loving those I have placed in your life. The forces of evil are great in the earth today. Love is waxing cold, but by My Spirit you can melt what is frozen, and you can restore the love I have placed within them, for Me and for My people. Encourage them not to give up that love.

Others are fainting in the day of adversity and their strength is low. They have been struggling to believe. Tell them to look to Me as their strength and rejoice in

Me because I am stronger than anything they will ever face.

I will take them by the hand and lead them on the path they should follow. Their life will be renewed as they wait upon Me, as they praise and worship Me.

I HAVE THE REMEDY

Encourage people to remember all the good I have done for them. When they are thankful, their strength will once again return because their thoughts will be on Me, not on themselves. They will rise again and finish what I have begun.

Others are suffering sickness, maladies, and diseases which are upon the earth. Discouragement abounds because there is no hope, no help, no cure. Yet I have the remedy for every illness.

There is no disease that has more power than I have. Help My people to believe in Me and hold fast, not to look at the symptoms or what is happening in their minds or bodies, but to know My healing anointing is greater.

*As they search their hearts and draw
near to Me, I will heal them. For I am
Jehovah Raffa, the Lord that healeth thee.
There is nothing too difficult for Me.*

So inspire My people to hold on and believe Me. I

am with them, and I will help them.

As I have taken care of you, now you can help those who I place in your path, and who are around you. I will lead you to them and they will be strengthened, loved, and empowered.

I WILL BE THERE

Many feel rejected and do not know where to turn. Tell them that in their day of trouble, I will be there.

Others are receiving the bounty of earth, yet they do not remember from whence the blessings came. Tell them to return to their first love and not be distracted by material possessions or earthly honors. They will say, "Thank you for reminding me of all the good the Lord has done for me. I thank and praise His Holy Name."

Tell people what great and
Wonderful things you have seen,
And what you know to be true.
Encourage them,
For they need to know I do
The things I say I will do.

They will be inspired to have hope, faith, and love because they know these will not fail.

WE WILL CLAIM VICTORY

I am your help in times of trial. When the world is

in conflict, I will display My glory. Where there is strife, invite my Spirit to come upon the scene. Know today that together we will claim victory.

Bring My Spirit into the situation and I will be glorified and honored. Stand back and watch what I will do. I will show myself mighty in behalf of those who put their trust and confidence in Me.

I will not only set you free, but liberate others through you. No longer are you weak, helpless and alone, for I am in you and upon you.

My anointing and My Word are mighty.
They are one.
I am with you,
And you have already won.

HOLD FAST

Be of good cheer. I, the Lord your God, go ahead of you to prepare the way. Don't be afraid or dismayed, and certainly don't give up. Remember this. As you continue in My Word you will know the truth—it will make and keep you free. You have the victory!

There are some who say, "This was just for yesterday."

I say to you, yes, this was for yesterday, but it is also for today, and will be until I come again. So hold fast to what I have given in the past and the present, for I will prevail forever.

YOUR HOPE LIES AHEAD

I have not asked you do to My work in all places. You can only be faithful to the assignment I have given you where you are. Be content, thankful and put your heart into what you are doing.

I take pleasure in My work and will help you to *know* your part and *do* your part. You will be faithful, complete the task and will receive the crown of life and blessing that I have prepared for you. It will be a day of great rejoicing among My people.

When things seem estranged on this earth, keep your hope focused on what lies ahead—no one can take your vision away from you.

Hold fast to Me. I will see you through to the victory, to all I have intended for your life and My kingdom. You are but a small part of the whole, but you are an important part. You are precious to Me, and I care about what you do, because I do it *through* you.

THEY WILL SPEAK THE TRUTH

The days of caring are not over, but My people will become more mature. They will not be operating out of their emotions, but will speak the truth in love and in the boldness found in the Spirit in the heart of God. As a result, My people will grow and enter into all I have purposed and planned.

Those who need a touch from God will come
From the north, south, east and west.
They will come, they will hunger for Me,
And they will know, yes,
I am the One who can set them free.
They will know I am the healer and the deliverer.
I am the mighty One of Israel.
I am the One of the Word who has done
things past, present and future.
I do not change.
Be encouraged and rejoice again.
Be glad; don't dwell on past mistakes.
It's time to move on and to win.

PUT AWAY DISTRACTIONS

I make a way and I open a door no one can shut. I do not go where there is emptiness. I do not spend my time in vanity, futile pursuits or insignificant matter with no purpose.

They are distractions. Put them out of your life, for they stand in the way of My purpose and plan for My kingdom.

I AM FORMING A MIGHTY ARMY

I will draw people of My Spirit, saith the Lord. They will seek My face and desire Me with all their hearts. They will come into My presence with gladness and joy, for they are seeking My Kingdom.

They desire the things of God, the Word, the truth, the power and the wisdom of God, and they want to walk in My ways. They will not entertain anything of the flesh, the world, or of another spirit.

I am asking you to put your arms around these people, yet you will not need to coddle them as a child. They will stand strong with you, for I am sending them by My Spirit. I am forming a mighty army.

Yes, care for the young ones, but know this: your time will be spent with those who walk with Me, know My voice, and hear My voice. They will be the ones with whom you will work together.

You will see My purpose and My plan come to fruition.

Encourage My people this day.

TWELVE

BE READY FOR A TRIUMPHANT DAY

For the Lord himself will come down from heaven, with a loud command, with the voice of the archangel and with the trumpet call of God, and the dead in Christ will rise first. After that, we who are still alive and are left will be caught up together with them in the clouds to meet the Lord in the air. And so we will be with the Lord forever. Therefore encourage each other with these words.
– 1 THESSALONIANS 4:16-18

I renew this promise to you this day that I will establish My Kingdom, and make clear My purpose.

Those who seek Me with all their hearts will find Me, and I will cause great and wonderful things to happen despite what is going on around them or to them.

My purpose will be ordained and will come to pass in behalf of those who seek Me. They will sing forth My praises. All will know I am a God who loves My people and delights in those who seek and believe in Me.

I GIVE YOU HANDS TO SERVE

I have given you a voice that you might speak my words, My wisdom, My knowledge and understanding. I have given you eyes so you might see the revelation of My Spirit, the works that I do and the truth in which I perform them.

I've given you ears that you might hear what the Spirit of the Lord has to say—and to hear the cries of the people and their needs.

I have given you hands to serve Me—to work, help, heal and assist Me in fulfilling my work here on earth. I flow through you, saith the Lord.

───────── ✦ ─────────

*I have given you feet to walk My ways,
to go to places that I have directed.*

My Spirit is upon you with great and mighty wisdom and power. At times you may have thought you failed, yet in your weakness My strength was perfected. I allowed this so you would know that I alone am the Lord your God. In only Me can you rely and place your trust.

Let me say to you again that I anticipate blessing for your life. I give you a hope and a reason to rejoice in your time of need. You will know I am the One who pours favor upon you, before you, and have hedged you in with blessing. You are surrounded by My love.

JOY WILL BE ON YOUR LIPS

As you walk in My way, I will restore what was lost and heal what has been hurt. I will remove the pain and the sorrow you have experienced. I will cause you to be glad in Me. You will not remember the former things, for they will no longer have power over you.

You will have gladness of heart and joy will be found on your lips. As people look into your eyes, they will see the hope I have placed within you, a hope which says, "Yes, my God whom I trust is able. He is able."

I will say through you, "Yes, mighty is the Lord your God."

Be confident in the ways that I have set before you. Though the road may be hard and the journey long, I am there with you every step of the way.

Do not discard your faith or hope, and trust only in Me.

YOU HAVE MY RESURRECTION POWER

As you reflect back and remember the things I have

blessed you with, you will be filled with hope again. Refreshing will come. Strength I will multiply within you; and you will rise up as out of the ashes.

You will see the victory of God, for My resurrection power rests upon and within you. The same mighty power I used to raise your Lord Jesus from the dead, I have within you.

There are those who will push you down, but I will cause you to rise even higher. In the world you will have tribulation, but fear not, I have overcome the world, saith the Lord.

Let the triumph and confidence rise within you which says, I will not be defeated. I will not be cast down. I will not be depressed. I will not be caught off guard. It may have happened before, but it will not occur again.

The Lord is saying, "Call unto Me in the day of trouble and I will deliver you. I will help you."

DO NOT LOSE FAITH

I have a great future for you, saith the Lord. I desire for you to prosper, to be in good health, to see the blessing that I have intended for your life, and not only for you, but for everyone.

If what you envision does not transpire, do not lose faith. Though the vision tarry, it is for an appointed time; it will happen.

You will see the desire I have placed in your heart come to light. It is for a specific moment. You will see it if you faint not and only believe

YOU WILL FEAR NO EVIL

The thief has set ambushes in many places, but by My Spirit I am going ahead of you and will clear your path. The demons which would attack you have no power unless you give it to them. Do not acknowledge their presence; they are only a fleeting shadow and my Spirit has already dealt with them.

For your purpose they are dead and will not influence your future.

―――――― ⟫―――――

You are precious in My sight,
and I am taking care of you.

Just keep moving forward, and though you walk through the valley of the shadow of death, you will fear no evil, for I am with you. I will not leave you or forsake you. Know this: surely goodness and mercy will follow you all the days of your life.

THE FLESH CANNOT STAY

Hate that which is tainted by the flesh; do not even spend one moment allowing people to hold on to what is not pure and true. Rebuke and remove what is defiled, for it must be driven away. That spirit does not understand caring, kindness, mercy, compassion and love, for it knows nothing of such things. It came to steal, kill and destroy.

————— ❧ —————

Love My people,
But drive those influences of the flesh,
Of the world, and of the demonic order away.
They have no place where My Spirit is,
And they cannot stay.
Those who wish to have them stay, must go.
They are not of My Spirit,
And they must be driven away.

When you speak "I believe," you bring what I have done in the Spirit realm into the physical realm. This is why I have declared, "When you pray, believe you have received, and you will see it happen."

If you believe Me, you will behold the manifestation of My glory. You will see My promise come to pass for you.

YOU WILL NOT NEED A SIGN

People are always looking for confirmation—a sign. "Oh, show me something."

When I walked the earth, it was the same, but even if they had seen a sign, they would not have believed. This is why I say, "Trust Me, believe Me, and you will see My works."

You will not need signs, for you will enjoy the reality. You will have Me.

I left the earth and sent My Spirit, who is here with you now. To those who believe, the works I do, you will also do—and even greater than these will you perform, because I have gone to the Father.

I am going to return, saith the Lord. So prepare your hearts. I am coming, and you will not know the hour.

Be ready, and we will be together forever. I look forward to that glorious day when you will behold Me face to face. You will know Me as I know you.

I WILL NOT DELAY

I have great anticipation for the moment when you will behold My glory as never before.

The evil one I will send away, and there will be no more sickness, pain, suffering, delusions, falsehood, lies, deceit, poverty, pestilence, famines, depression, anxiety, worries and hopelessness. No more confusion, unbelief, or death.

How I long in My heart for you to have all I have prepared for you.

In that day you will enjoy the pleasures of My presence forevermore.

Love and care for My people, for I am coming soon. I will not tarry. Tell them to be ready for the greatest, most extravagant time they will ever witness. I will arrive in triumph.

Tell people of My love, and invite them to be with Me.

THIRTEEN

THE BEST IS YET TO COME

Eye hath not seen, nor ear heard, neither have
entered into the heart of man, the things which God
hath prepared for them that love him.
— 1 CORINTHIANS 2:9 KJV

My substance is coming to My people, saith the Lord. I am sending it even now.

Those who have their hearts set to receive will see, for it is on the way. So prepare yourselves through thanksgiving to welcome the blessing with praise.

Eagerly desire and seek Me so you will know what to do with what I am giving you, the substance I supply.

Blessed are they who call upon the name of the Lord, for they shall not go away empty-handed. They shall receive the increase I provide. They will never lack or have reason to beg for any good thing.

You will have *more* than enough to share with others, that they too might receive the goodness of My storehouse through you.

Those who call to Me and request to be a source of My provision, I will use on earth as I did with Joseph, My son. He supplied the people of the earth in their day of hunger through My wisdom. Yes, in the time of plenty, he knew how to prepare and save. Then, when the years of famine came, the people still had plenty.

MY BEST WILL BE YOURS

The days of lack will fall upon the earth. Those who put their trust in Me, rely upon and use My provision as I direct, will never have need, saith the Lord.

Be wise managers of that which I provide.

I say unto you,
I desire great and wonderful things for you,
My children.
I desire that My best come to you,
All the things from heaven.
You will know what is right and fresh,
What is new, and good, and what is leaven.
You will know what is
Blessed and what is cursed.
You will say, "I want what is blessed all my days.
For surely goodness and mercy
Shall follow me all my days,
And I will dwell in the house of the Lord forever.
Though I walk through the valley of the shadow of death,

I will not fear, for I know my God is here.
Yes, He is so dear, I will draw near.
I will hunger and thirst for Him
As the deer pants for the water.
I will draw near to my God in whom I receive,
And I give honor.
Glory to the name of the Lord Most High.
Upon Him I delight.
I thank Him as I draw nigh.
Yes, near and close is what I want to be,
For in You, Lord, is my trust.
And it's in You that I am free.
Free to be all that You have intended me to be.
I Thank You."

THE TABLE IS SPREAD

If you are faithful with a little, I will give you increase. Yes, more and more. My resources are limitless. They only cease when you do not believe, or look to another source.

When you go to a banquet and everything is prepared, you are a guest there to enjoy, not to wonder what you should bring or what you should do.

I have spread the table for you. All things are ready and waiting. All I am asking is that you come to the feast and delight in My presence.

When you enter the king's courts, the king takes care of all things. I am the King of kings, the Lord of lords, and there is none like unto Me. So trouble not yourself, but enjoy the abundant life I have supplied for you through My Son, Jesus.

I have made you royal priests and kings and extended to you My blessing. Do not speak contrary to the abundance I have placed upon your life. You speak the truth when you declare, "I am blessed of the Lord."

LOOK AHEAD!

Enjoy what I have prepared; it will not be taken away. I care for you and will increase the supply. You will have sufficiency at all times to give wherever I direct and lead. I am using you to fulfill what I want accomplished in the earth.

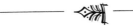

People say, "Who am I? What am I about?
What am I to do?"
And I say to them,
I know who you are and I know what you are to do.
Ask me, I will show and tell you,
Then you will see.
You will know who you are, and what you will be.
I know your beginning, I know where you live.
I know where you're going, I know where you've been.
I say to you, look ahead,
Don't look back, for that's not where you live.
Look ahead.
Understand, I'm there with you.
I'm walking with you. I'm talking with you.

Look ahead and be glad.
For you're not dead, you're alive.
You're alive forevermore
Because of the One that you adore...
The Lord Jesus.

I Am The True Treasure

Remove the spirit of poverty from your life.

Those who lack are those who do not obey Me; follow My ways and listen to My direction. I will not help those who do not rely upon Me or go contrary to My will.

They will fail because I will oppose those who are proud in My sight and who lean to their own understanding. I will not allow their sinful ways to prosper.

Do not envy those who do things in opposition to My will, yet seem to have success. Do not think they are prospering and blessed, for the day will come when everything will be shown for what it is. They will fail and fall.

Their possessions will come to nothing, for the moth creates holes in the garment. The things of the earth decay and pass away, yet what I provide remains forever.

Many have earthly treasures, yet they do not have My blessing, for they are not rich toward me. They cannot receive My supply because they have not sought Me with all their hearts. This is why I say,

"Let them give up what they have and seek Me, for I am the true treasure."

ENJOY MY PRESENCE

I create zeal for My Word in the hearts of My people. I plant a craving, a longing, a desire for My presence. Once they have a touch of what I am speaking of, even now, they will never desire to return to their old pleasures.

Enjoy My presence, for I am here. I am with you. Rest in My peace, joy and the quietness I supply to you.

I HAVE BETTER THINGS IN STORE

If you are not ashamed to confess Me before people, I am not ashamed to confess you. I will announce, "There is My son; there is My daughter." Yes, child, you have had your days of struggle, but know you are Mine.

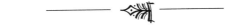

You will always come back to what I have planned, provided and purposed for you.

When moments of heaviness fall, realize they come because you are unfulfilled. You are empty. I destined you to be full of My presence—My substance—and I have better things in store.

I AM YOUR SOURCE

Never set your affections on the fleeting things of this earth. They cannot fill or sustain you. Without me all is nothing. I am your source of abundant life.

What are accomplishments and achievements without Me? They are as a vapor. Your life is a whisper in the wind.

Whether you live or die, you live again. I've conquered and I have won, so do not even hold on to your life. It is not yours to save; it's Mine.

I have amazing things in store for you that you have not seen or planned. It is coming. So welcome, anticipate, praise and give thanks. I have everything under control.

The best is yet to come!

FOURTEEN

MY GIFT WILL SHINE THROUGH YOU

*...the nations will know that I am
the Lord...when I show myself holy
through you before their eyes.*
– EZEKIEL 36:23

When My people call, I answer. I embrace them with an everlasting love that cannot change.

All I ask is for you to simply believe, for when you do, you trust and obey Me.

Tell the spirit of despair, "You don't belong here." Confront the spirit of confusion and say, "Clarity reigns in this place," and confusion will flee.

YOU ARE A NEW CREATION

Every time we are together, I tell you how much I love you, saith the Lord.

What does love do? It thinks love, speaks love and acts love. I do good because I *am* good—and I have made you to be in My image. Since I am love, so are you.

It is not for you to judge, find fault, manipulate, or seek to control. This never brings about My changes or results in My ways.

At one time you were consumed with your own lusts and desires, but no more. I have made you to be a new creation, a chosen child of the Most High God, with a purpose and a destiny to show forth My praises in the earth—to do good, to destroy the work of the devil. My Spirit will do this through you, as you are good, gentle, patient and tolerant.

The reason you came to Me is because I was all of these things to you. My loving kindness wooed you into My presence. You began to realize there was something lacking—and that was Me.

Your spirit became alive to Me as I intended from the beginning of time.

The old has passed away.
It has no power to stay.
Don't allow it to come back. It has no place.
Don't give it an entrance or way.

MAN'S WAYS ARE NOT MY WAYS

You once walked in vanity, emptiness and folly—the harvest of futile thinking.

Those days are over. They never accomplished

anything you wanted them to.

What the world refers to as wise, I regard as foolishness. And what the world despises, I love.

Man's ways are not My ways, saith the Lord. And those who walk in such paths will not comprehend, appreciate or even desire the things of Me. Why? They have eyes, but do not see. They have ears, yet do not hear. They are blind to what I have prepared. But those who come to Me I will not turn away.

YOUR GIFT IS SPECIAL

Do not throw pearls before people who are not ready to receive, lest the gift becomes too common. When they desire excellence, then is the time.

It is the pearl of great price that a person is willing to give up everything for.

Are you not of high value? Don't give yourself where you're not appreciated, desired, or wanted, for then you will be demeaned, disgraced and held in shame.

No, by My Spirit, there is a right time and a right place for My gift to shine forth. It will be wanted, needed—and very special.

I AM POSITIONING YOU

Develop the gift I have placed within you, for I am

mobilizing My people. I'm raising them up and positioning them throughout the earth for My purpose and My glory. I am placing them in neighborhoods, families, communities and nations to let My light shine throughout the earth. Allow Me to position you.

Do not scurry to and fro saying, "This is my gift."

If you operate in this manner, people will not even recognize your calling. Rather, they will say, "How conceited, how rude!"

They will miss the destiny and purpose I have given you. Let Me do the promoting. Allow Me to build the platform for My gift to radiate through you.

*Your assignment is to be available
and develop what I have placed within you.*

WHAT DO YOU FEEL DRAWN TO?

You may wonder, "What is my gift?"

Look at your life. Your gift is the thing you love to do. I place the desire within you—that is why you feel drawn to it.

Do you delight in encouraging people? Do you enjoy creating and designing? Do you have organizational skills? One specific vision is your calling.

Let me give you this word of caution. The place of your gift will also be the site of your opposition, for the evil one intends to steal your talent and make you question, "Oh, I have no gift."

In truth, it is just the opposite—this is where your gift shines the brightest.

If your passion is to minister, and you see someone in need, there will be the moment to ask, "How can I help you?"

There is also a time to be quiet. Always be available and allow your gift to make its own way—and to respond when it is needed.

BE PATIENT AND PREPARE

Cleanse your heart, mind and body from anything pertaining to self. Then the gift can flow through a clean vessel to honor Me.

Every purpose has a plan and a preparation time. Don't be in a rush, because the gift in the wrong place, at the wrong time, to the wrong people will not be welcomed or appreciated. Nor will it be a blessing.

I make all things beautiful in My timing.

Be patient. Prepare. Receive the plan and know there is a purpose. I am not in a hurry, and you cannot fulfill your calling without Me.

I am the gift, saith the Lord. And because I dwell in you, it makes you a gift also.

There will be a time when we will brightly shine together.

FIFTEEN

STEP OUT IN FAITH

Have faith in the Lord your God and
you will be upheld; have faith in his prophets
and you will be successful.
– 2 CHRONICLES 20:20

S and shifts and the earth shakes. The day will come when the heavens and the world will tremble and be consumed with fire.

Look around, you can see the signs. Everything is being torn asunder except what is rooted and anchored in Me. I am the only One you can rely upon, for I neither shift or move.

Place your trust in Me, not in the uncertainty of this world. I am solid and sure—the Lord who will never change.

Feelings fluctuate, circumstances are unpredictable and people alter their positions. Nothing remains the same except Me.

I bring life and I give life, and whoever believes in

119

Me, though he die, yet shall he live.

Place your total trust in Me. Be confident and assured, for I am the Rock of your salvation. You shall not be moved.

RISE UP!

Arise and stand tall. Receive what the Spirit of the Lord is giving you this day. I call to the earth and say, "Rise up, My people. Be glorified in My Name and know that I the Lord never change. What I have said I will surely do, for I am the Lord your God."

I hasten to perform My Word
On behalf of those who call upon My name.
They will never be the same,
For I will cause them to be changed.

When My transformation takes place in you, a new day will dawn. You will be fresh, washed, cleansed, and forgiven; you will be My holy people.

I will cause the new heaven and the new earth to come forth. What has been will be no more because what I bring forth is permanent.

- Have I healed you? Then you are healed.
- Have I saved you? Then you are saved.
- Have I delivered you? Then you are delivered.

120

Lift up holy hands and be glad. Do not receive an evil report, for I am your confidence. I never, never change.

SAFE AND SECURE

The world cannot offer what I bring. Why? Because it is of shifting sands and unstable. It is moving on an unsteady course and knows not where it is headed.

Keep your trust in Me and stay grounded in faith. Do not be affected by what you see and hear in these ungodly days. Let My Spirit bring you back to a place where you are safe and secure—at home in My everlasting arms.

A NEW SONG

As you lift your voice to Me, My song will burst forth—and it will bring blessings. For I sing over you with joy and confidence. It is a song of peace the world does not know, but I give it to those who call upon My Name. Those who come into My presence I fill with My gladness.

The peace I bring,
Will cause you to sing,
A new song to the Lord.
For I have put it within you.

The song is even now on your lips.

121

So be refreshed. Things which have become old, tired and worn I am making brand new. I am restoring joy into your heart and mind.

You may have been troubled by this world, but fear not, I have overcome the world.

Put away the cares of this life, for you are now in My presence. Remember, you are not of this world; you are of My Spirit. My Kingdom is here within you now, but soon it will be everywhere.

There will be no more evil, pain or sorrow, for My Spirit will reign, and My people will behold Me. We will fellowship with one another face to face.

Now you don't see Me, but the day will soon come when You will. You will look upon Me, and no other, for I will enthrall your heart. I will be all you need.

WAVES OF REFRESHING

Enjoy My presence, for I am with you and will never forsake you. Always, you will be in My presence, for I am within. You will know the goodness of the Lord, for My Spirit will prevail upon you time and again.

Over and over, just as waves crash upon the shore, times of refreshing will come without ceasing. You will say, "Thank You, Lord. May it never end."

It will never pass away, for I love you with an everlasting love.

Look not to another, because nothing can fill your life so completely. You were created for Me.

The time of renewal is now. Receive from Me what you need. My refreshing will be as a cool glass of water on a hot day.

When you drink freely of My water of life, you will never, ever thirst again.

BE READY

I will lead you to people and people to you. I will show you what to do, bringing together the ingredients that are necessary. Be ready. Prepare your heart and mind, for the time is at hand.

———— ⟨≫⟩ ————

The steps of the righteous
Are ordered of the Lord.
Though they stumble,
They will not be utterly cast down or uprooted.
They will not be abhorred,
For the blessing of God is upon their lives.
They will stand up again by God's mighty hand,
And say, "I am free from strife.
I will not go there again.
I will not enter in."
Those ways, saith the Lord, are not My ways.
They have hindered My people
From having blessed and wonderful days.

MOVE FORWARD

I am asking you to step out in faith and go.

"Go where?" you ask.

I will show you and there will be inner peace about the direction.

Don't ponder over the decision or worry if it is the right path. Trust Me and boldly move forward.

Go, and I will show,
What you need to know.
Be not afraid to dream.
Believe, hope, and go.
I will be with you
And will show you the way.

TIME IS SHORT

Learn My ways. You have heard that I am meek, gentle, patient, kind and humble of heart. It is also said I am longsuffering. Many dislike this word, believing if they follow Me they will have to suffer long.

Understand this: time is short. Yes, tribulation comes, but when you suffer for Me, My blessing and glory rests upon you. You will be rejoicing in My Spirit.

I will come upon you in such a mighty way,
You will not even understand or comprehend
What's happening on that day.

This great joy will come to you,
And won't depart.
The peace of God will guard and keep you,
In your mind and heart.
You will say, "This is wonderful"
And others will look at you and wonder,
"What? Have you gone crazy this day?"
You will say, "No, I'm doing it the Lord's way.
God is for me, so who can be against me?"
Then you will declare,
"Yes, my God is mighty, He loves me,
And He shows it in this way."

Others may reject you and say what is cruel, but I will flood your soul with sweet words of encouragement, kindness, strength, mercy and love.

The world is waiting for you to deliver My message. Step out in faith today.

SIXTEEN

A NEW DAY HAS BEGUN

...his compassions never fail. They are
new every morning; great is your faithfulness.
– LAMENTATIONS 3:22-23

Birth pangs mean something is being born. Though it starts small, what I create will grow and thrive.

Remember your humble beginnings and trust me in those times. What I am birthing is new and fresh and even what is old is being reborn. I am giving new meaning, new direction, new purpose and new life.

ALIVE AGAIN

Learn to see through My eyes. In the cold of winter many things seem dead, yet it is only in appearance. When springtime arrives they burst alive again. At first there will be one leaf, then two. Next comes the bud, then flowers and fruit. Whatever God plans and intends, that is what it becomes.

I am the God of the living. Those who die in Me are not dead, they live forevermore. As I said, "Today you will be with Me in Paradise."

The opposite is also true. Those without Me appear to be alive, yet they are dead.

How much better it is to draw near to Me and become born again—and begin a new, exciting life. This is why I tell My people, let everything that has breath praise the Lord.

DON'T GIVE UP

It is easy to praise Me when things go well, but in *all* circumstances, at all times, give thanks. I am greater than any situation you are facing. I birthed you and you are My child, therefore I will help you in your hour of trouble.

Be happy and glad because the way has been shown. Believe and walk on my road. I will light the way as you take each step—and I will cause you to succeed.

Don't give up and don't give in,
Saith the Lord.
For the battle we will win.

YOU WILL TRIUMPH

My Spirit is upon My people, and I cause My power and might to rise up within them. They are My children who will stand and overcome. They will triumph and see the victory of their God.

They will raise their voices and shout for joy, "Yes, this is truly the day of redemption and the blessing of the Lord."

Provision is on the way, and I tell my people to declare, "My God reigns! He is able to do all things. My God reigns!"

Your tears will change from those of sorrow and desperation to tears of joy. Thankfulness will rise within your heart and you will worship and praise My Holy Name.

My people will stand and declare,
"The Lord has blessed me richly on every side."

EVERY KNEE SHALL BOW

I am raising up people who are called by My Name, who will pray, intercede, stand in the gap and prepare the way for My great and glorious return.

I will arrive crowned in glory, honor and power. Everyone will acknowledge I am their God, for there is none like unto Me. Every knee shall bow, every tongue will confess that I am the Lord. I will cause My people to be established forever.

I WILL FORGIVE

Those who have loved Me and have kept My

commandments, I will love—and they will love Me. Together, we will live forevermore in peace and harmony.

Those who have been incensed against you
Will fall by the side.
For they have not called upon My Name,
Nor in My word do they abide.

Because they have sought others and looked to themselves rather than honoring Me, they have cut themselves off from blessing. Yet, I am ready to forgive them if they call on Me. I will grant them the same new life I have given unto you.

Even now, My Spirit flows in you and through you to reach out and touch those who need My love:

- I care for and delight in them.
- I rejoice over them with singing.
- I shout the voice of triumph over them.
- I command blessing upon them for they are My own.

I know both their weakness and their strength and am waiting to help those who seek Me with all their hearts.

THEY WILL SEE MY GLORY
My hand of favor, strength, wisdom, understanding

and blessing is upon you. Use these to reach out to those I love.

The wayward are returning. They are realizing their lives have been so empty. I am drawing them by My Spirit, so welcome them with open arms.

I have been answering your prayers that they come into all I have intended. Continue to thank Me in advance that none of them will be lost—that everyone you have committed to Me will return.

They will all see the glory of God. Not one will be lost. Hallelujah!

I have declared and this I will honor. I have promised, and I will fulfill, for I do the things I say.

Since they are not asking for themselves, please ask on their behalf. I will give them life and help them to do what is right.

In this way I will glorify Myself.

I never give up on anyone and I am asking you to do the same.

IT HAS BEGUN

I will do what you cannot accomplish by yourself. Let me help you, saith the Lord.

Consider it done—a new beginning has already begun. Be patient as I complete My perfect work.

It has begun, and it will work
Where it has not worked before.

131

You've tried so hard, and all was forlorn.
It came to nothing but pain and harm.
Sorrow was spread all around.
But now My Spirit has come to you
And said the joy will be found.
The hope will come, the peace will rise,
And joy beyond all measure.
For My Spirit has done what you could not do
For I will do it without measure.
I'll hold back nothing, saith the Lord.
I will do it. It is begun.
So rejoice and be glad, for you have won.

YOU ARE BECOMING LIKE ME

The reason you can triumph is because I have won the battle for you. So don't sorrow or be heavy-laden with burdens. Raise your hands high and shout to the Lord, "We have taken the ground. We've taken back what was stolen and received what God has given. And now it is ours to give again."

The love, peace, joy and hope I have placed in your hands is only the start of a great work I have begun in you—and I am still working!

Rise up, and become everything I have destined you to be, for My labor of love in your behalf has not been for nothing. It is succeeding and prospering.

You are growing into all I have intended; you are

becoming like Me.

WE WILL SEE VICTORY

Do not harden your heart, become stubborn or allow anything to hinder what I am doing with you and those around you. Rather, praise and thank Me—not only for my favor to you, but the blessings I am pouring out on those you have never met.

Every good thing will be both yours and theirs. Someday when you stand before Me you will know that many are here because of the grace and mercy you believed Me for on their behalf.

They will say the same about you. Together My people and I will see the victory of God. They will be honored on that day.

So forget the past; a glorious new day has begun!

SEVENTEEN

REJOICE IN ME!

Rejoice in the Lord always.
I will say it again: Rejoice!
– PHILIPPIANS 4:4

Let the shouts of triumph and praise flow from your lips, for you are confident in Me.

You know how all things do work together for good to them that love Me and are called according to My purpose.

You have prayed. Now believe you will receive and see it happen.

Let your spirit rise and soar. May you delight in Me, for I have spoken and have performed what I promised. Stand strong together in the faith. I am with you always.

I will cause My provision to come
From sources that you know not of.
You do not see them,
For they will be from above.

Rejoice and be glad!

WALK IN MY PRESENCE

Because you have set your love upon Me, I will rescue you. I will save, heal and deliver. I will give you long life and every blessing.

Know what the Spirit of the Lord has said to you this day. Walk in My presence and experience the fullness of joy.

YOUR BURDENS WILL BE LIFTED

It is time to press into the mark of the high calling of God which is yours in Me. You will rise up and celebrate.

My strength and wisdom will fall upon you. Your burdens will be lifted because I am greater than your circumstances.

Will you rejoice and comfort in Me, or will you act as those who have no faith, hope or love?

What will you do? How will you be?
How will you respond? What will you see?
What will you say? What will you do?
I know. Do you?

SEASONS OF REFRESHING

When I say I love you with an everlasting love that

136

never fades or changes, do I lie? Or do I speak the truth?

I am asking you to proclaim, "I am greatly loved of the Lord. I know in whom I have believed and I am fully persuaded and convinced He is able to keep that which I've committed to Him. So, if My God has everything under control, then I am going to rejoice in the Lord."

Seasons of refreshing will flow.
Whatever is not of Me, will have to go.

PEACE WILL INCREASE

The joy I have placed in your heart will grow even greater. The peace I give will increase.

My Spirit rests mightily upon you. It will daily be renewed and refreshed. As you think my thoughts there will be no weakness, no failure or lack of any good thing.

Be encouraged in your spirit,
Be encouraged in your mind.
Be refreshed in your body.
Life is truly sublime.

I give you only understanding, wisdom, power, peace and joy.

137

I SENT MY ANGELS

Be not concerned over circumstances. You will overcome and endure.

I did not find fault with My servant Elijah
When he feared and ran for his life.
I just told him, "Come out of the cave.
I'm not in the whirlwind, nor in the big fire.
I am in that still, small voice
Which you really desire."
I sought him out and loved him,
I encouraged him along the way.
I sent My angels, but he didn't listen
To what they had to say.
But I continued with him.
He went in the cave; I stayed outside,
For I don't need to run and hide.

I AM GUIDING

When Elijah became still within himself, then he heard My voice again. He yielded to My Spirit. He knew I loved him; he came out of the cave, and listened to what I had to say.

I told him not about his faults,
About his lack or his need.

138

I did not spend time telling him
He was deceived.
I did not find fault with him at that point in time.
I loved him, and I told him, "You've got time.
To do what I want you to do."

I continued, "Go. We have things to do and people to see. I am leading, guiding and directing."

He forgot the lies and was inspired to once again proclaim My Name.

MIRACLES WILL FLOW

There have been things which have prevented My Spirit from flowing freely, but I have cleansed and prepared this vessel. It is holy and blessed and My Spirit will increase in the days ahead.

Miracles of healing will flow again. There will be liberty and freedom.

So rejoice and be glad in everything this day,
And understand, I am on the way.
I am coming. I am coming soon.
Be ready for Me whether it is morning or noon,
The time is now at hand I say:
Rejoice in Me always.

I STAND AT THE DOOR

Rise up. I have a plan and a purpose for your life. Put aside the strife and bitterness.

Even now, I stand at the door and knock. If you will seek, you will find. By my Spirit, the door will be opened. Enter into the joy of the Lord.

Except I build the house, they that labor, labor in vain. They rise up early; they stay up late, trying to succeed, yet they fail. Why? Because I am not part of the plan.

Oh, if people would only call upon Me. I will cause their purpose to come to pass.

When you walk in the Spirit of the living God,
I will flow.
And I will show you what you need to know.
Has the Lord not said it, and will He not do it?
Has He not promised, and will He not fulfill?
The time is near. The time is now.
Understand that I will show you how.

REJOICE! REJOICE!

I will fill the whole earth with My glory.

All the nations and people will know I am the Lord, and there is none like unto Me. They will set aside those things in which they have blindly placed their trust.

I can hear the sounds of worship and echoes of praise, for there is nothing to quench My Spirit.

You are My reason for rejoicing because you receive My love and believe My Word. The work I have begun I will complete. It is done. No one shall pluck you out of My hand.

Rejoice, and again I say rejoice!

FOR A COMPLETE LIST OF BOOKS AND
MINISTRY RESOURCES BY THE AUTHOR,
CONTACT:

Randy C. Brodhagen
Glory to God Ministries International
P. O. Box 4167
Palm Springs, CA 92263

Phone: 760-321-5222
Fax: 760-321-5773
Email: pastor@glorytogod.org
Internet: www.glorytogod.org